A WATERY WORLD

TAKING CARE OF THE OCEAN

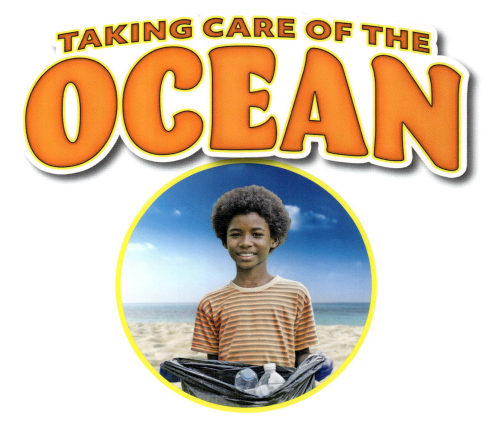

By Emma Carlson Berne

Consultant: Beth Gambro
Reading Specialist, Yorkville, Illinois

Minneapolis, Minnesota

Teaching Tips

Before Reading

- Look at the cover of the book. Discuss the picture and the title.
- Ask readers to brainstorm a list of what they already know about the ocean. What can they expect to see in the book?
- Go on a picture walk, looking through the pictures to discuss vocabulary and make predictions about the text.

During Reading

- Read for purpose. Encourage readers to think about how the ocean is important as they are reading.
- Ask readers to look for the details of the book. What are they learning about the things that hurt the ocean?
- If readers encounter an unknown word, ask them to look at the sounds in the word. Then, ask them to look at the rest of the page. Are there any clues to help them understand?

After Reading

- Encourage readers to pick a buddy and reread the book together.
- Ask readers to name two ways to help take care of the ocean. Find the pages that tell about these things.
- Ask readers to write or draw something they learned about taking care of the ocean.

Credits:

Cover and title page, © Amorn Suriyan/iStock and © icemanphotos/Adobe Stock; 3, © Inside Creative House/iStock; 5, © alxpin/iStock; 7, © Marina113/iStock; 8–9, © Damocean/iStock; 11, © twildlife/iStock; 12–13, © taylanibrahim/iStock; 15, © Zarina Lukash/iStock; 16–17, © MichaelUtech/iStock; 19, © Liderina/iStock; 21, © Godji10/iStock; 22T, © SolStock/iStock; 22M, © Cunaplus_M.Faba/iStock; 22B, © kali9/iStock; 23TL, © buzbuzzer/iStock; 23TR © goinyk/iStock; 23BL, © DavorLovincic/iStock; 23BR, © RainervonBrandis/iStock.

See BearportPublishing.com for our statement on Generative AI Usage.

Library of Congress Cataloging-in-Publication Data is available at www.loc.gov or upon request from the publisher.

ISBN: 979-8-88916-988-8 (hardcover)
ISBN: 979-8-89232-457-1 (paperback)
ISBN: 979-8-89232-093-1 (ebook)

Copyright © 2025 Bearport Publishing Company. All rights reserved. No part of this publication may be reproduced in whole or in part, stored in any retrieval system, or transmitted in any form or by any means, electronic, mechanical, photocopying, recording, or otherwise, without written permission from the publisher. Bearport Publishing is a division of Chrysalis Education Group.

For more information, write to Bearport Publishing, 5357 Penn Avenue South, Minneapolis, MN 55419.

Contents

Full of Life 4

You Can Help. 22

Glossary 23

Index 24

Read More 24

Learn More Online. 24

About the Author 24

Full of Life

Dolphins jump out of the water.

Green plants sway below the waves.

The ocean is full of life.

It is one of Earth's most important **habitats**!

Many plants and animals live in the ocean.

People get food from it.

How can we take care of the ocean?

Trash **pollutes** the ocean.

It makes the water dirty.

Plants and animals can get stuck in the trash.

Animals get hurt if they eat it.

Trash on the ground can end up in the ocean.

Putting it in trash cans helps keep the water clean.

Let's pick up the trash we see.

11

Many people eat fish.

We need to catch a lot.

Sometimes, we take too many fish from the water.

This is called **overfishing**.

Some fishers are careful not to overfish.

They make sure lots of fish are left in the water.

People burn **fuel** to make many things work.

This puts bad gases in the air.

It makes the ocean warmer.

This hurts animals.

Using less fuel can help the ocean.

We can walk or bike instead of riding in cars.

This beautiful water is important for all life on Earth.

Let's take care of the ocean together!

You Can Help

Taking care of the ocean is important. What can you do to help?

Use a water bottle that can be filled up again and again. This makes less trash.

Fuel gives us power for our homes. Turn off lights when you are not using them.

Talk to your friends and family about why the ocean is important. Share different ways they can help, too.

Glossary

fuel something that is burned to make power

habitats places in nature where plants and animals normally live

overfishing catching too many fish in one area

pollutes makes something dirty in a way that harms Earth

Index

animals 6, 8, 18
cars 18
fish 4, 12, 14
fuel 16, 18, 22
habitats 4
trash 8, 10, 22

Read More

Gulati, Annette. *Ocean Explorers (Starting with STEAM).* North Mankato, MN: Rourke Educational Media, 2020.

Thielges, Alissa. *In the Ocean (Spot Nature).* Mankato, MN: Amicus Learning, 2024.

Learn More Online

1. Go to **www.factsurfer.com** or scan the QR code below.
2. Enter "**Taking Care Ocean**" into the search box.
3. Click on the cover of this book to see a list of websites.

About the Author

Emma Carlson Berne lives with her family in Cincinnati, Ohio. She always recycles her plastics!